disc

Polygons

Marina Cohen

Crabtree Publishing Company

www.crabtreebooks.com

Author: Marina Cohen
Publishing plan research and development:
  Sean Charlebois, Reagan Miller
  Crabtree Publishing Company
Editor: Reagan Miller
Proofreader: Crystal Sikkens
Editorial director: Kathy Middleton
Project coordinator: Margaret Salter
Prepress technician: Margaret Salter
Coordinating editor: Chester Fisher
Series editor: Jessica Cohn
Project manager: Kumar Kunal (Q2AMEDIA)
Art direction: Cheena Yadav (Q2AMEDIA)
Cover design: Suzena Samuel(Q2AMEDIA)
Design: Divij Singh (Q2AMEDIA)
Photo research: Nivisha Sinha (Q2AMEDIA)

Photographs:
Dreamstime: Lawrence Weslowski Jr.: p. 1
Istockphoto: Dave White: p. 6, 11; Alexandra Draghici: p. 14 (left);
  Subjug: p. 14 (right); Mark Murphy: p. 15;
Photolibrary: Doug Menuez: p. 17 (bottom); Erik Isakson: p. 21 (top);
Q2AMedia Art Bank : Content Page, 4, 6, 7, 8, 9, 10, 11, 12, 13, 14, 16, 17,
  18, 19, 20, 22, 24
Other images by Shutterstock

Library and Archives Canada Cataloguing in Publication

Cohen, Marina
        Polygons / Marina Cohen.

(My path to math)
Includes index.
ISBN 978-0-7787-6784-8 (bound).--ISBN 978-0-7787-6793-0 (pbk.)

        1. Polygons--Juvenile literature. I. Title. II. Series: My path to math

QA482.C64 2010   j516'.154   C2010-900821-9

Library of Congress Cataloging-in-Publication Data

Cohen, Marina, 1967-
  Polygons / Marina Cohen.
    p. cm. -- (My path to math)
  Includes index.
  ISBN 978-0-7787-6784-8 (reinforced lib. bdg. : alk. paper) -- ISBN 978-0-7787-
6793-0 (pbk. : alk. paper)
  1. Polygons--Juvenile literature. 2. Geometry, Plane--Juvenile literature. 3.
  Baseball--Juvenile literature. I. Title. II. Series.

  QA482.C64 2011
  516'.154--dc22

                                                                            2010003030

Crabtree Publishing Company

Printed in China/082010/AP20100512

www.crabtreebooks.com   1-800-387-7650

Published in Canada
Crabtree Publishing
616 Welland Ave.
St. Catharines, ON
L2M 5V6

Published in the United States
Crabtree Publishing
PMB 59051
350 Fifth Avenue, 59th Floor
New York, New York 10118

Published in the United Kingdom
Crabtree Publishing
Maritime House
Basin Road North, Hove
BN41 1WR

Published in Australia
Crabtree Publishing
386 Mt. Alexander Rd.
Ascot Vale (Melbourne)
VIC 3032

Contents

Play Ball!

Emily and her dad are at a baseball game. There is a lot to see! She looks around and sees all kinds of shapes.

Dad tells Emily that some of the shapes are **polygons**. A polygon is a closed shape. A polygon has at least three **sides** that are straight.

The sides of a polygon are called **line segments**. Each line segment connects to other line segments to form a shape.

Activity Box

Sort the shapes. Which have at least three straight sides? Do the sides close completely? If so, those are polygons.

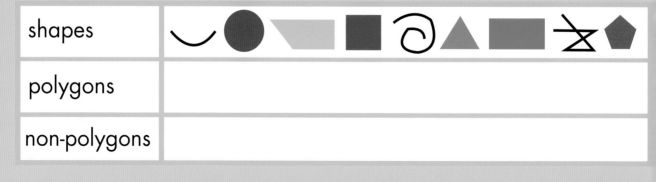

shapes	
polygons	
non-polygons	

Even the baseball field has shapes.

▼ baseball field

Go, Team!

Emily sees someone wave a flag showing the team's colors. The flag has straight sides. Its sides form a closed shape. It is a polygon called a triangle.

Dad explains that the names for polygons have to do with how many sides they have. *Tri* means "three." A triangle has three sides.

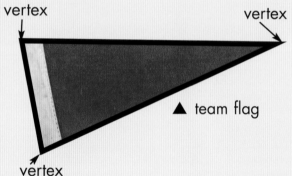

vertex

vertex

vertex

▲ team flag

All polygons have at least three sides. All polygons have at least three **vertices**, too. A **vertex** is like a corner. They are the **points** where two sides of a polygon meet.

Activity Box

This is an octagon. How many sides does it have? How many vertices does it have?

Which of these shapes do you already know?

polygons

	tri = 3 triangle three sides and three vertices
	quad = 4 quadrilateral four sides and four vertices
	pent = 5 pentagon five sides and five vertices
	hex = 6 hexagon six sides and six vertices
	hept = 7 heptagon seven sides and seven vertices

7

Angles

Dad asks Emily if she knows what an **angle** is. Each corner of a polygon forms an angle. The angles form where the line segments meet.

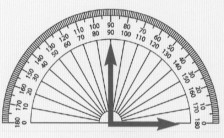

protractor ▲

A polygon has as many angles as it has sides. A polygon with three sides has three angles. A polygon with four sides has four angles.

We measure the angles by **degrees**. The degrees show the **width** of the angles.

Right angles are 90 degrees wide. **Acute angles** are smaller. They measure between 0 and 90 degrees. **Obtuse angles** are bigger. They measure between 90 and 180 degrees.

angles

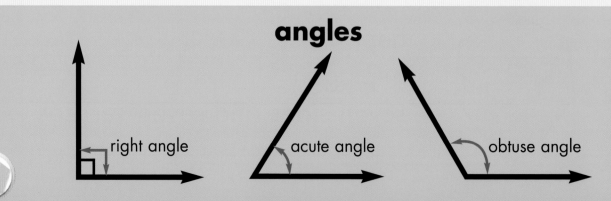

right angle   acute angle   obtuse angle

Dad says you can picture degrees as tiny slices of pie!

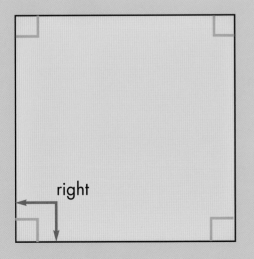

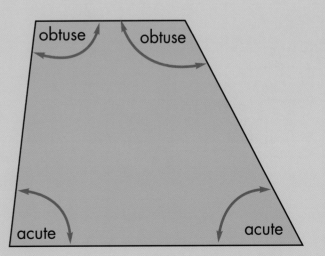

This polygon has four sides and four angles. The angles are all right angles.

This polygon has four sides and four angles. Two of the angles are obtuse and two are acute.

Triangles

Dad says that the sizes of the sides and angles are important. Triangles have three sides. They have three vertices and three angles. Triangles have these three things in common. Yet triangles take many shapes.

This triangle has two sides of the same **length**. It has two equal angles.

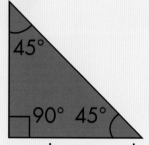

isosceles triangle

This triangle has three sides of the same length. It has three equal angles.

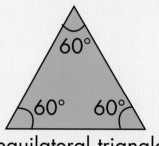

equilateral triangle

This triangle has no equal sides. It has no equal angles.

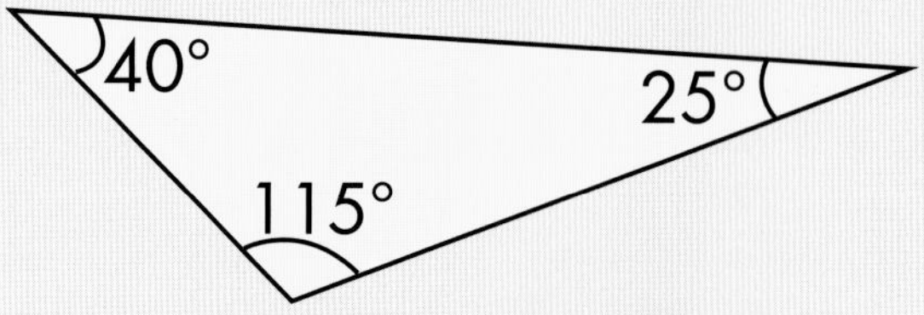

scalene triangle

Activity Box

Which triangle shown above has one obtuse angle?
Which triangle shown above has one right angle?

A flag like this is called a pennant. This one has two sides that are the same size. It has two equal angles. This flag forms an isosceles triangle.

triangle

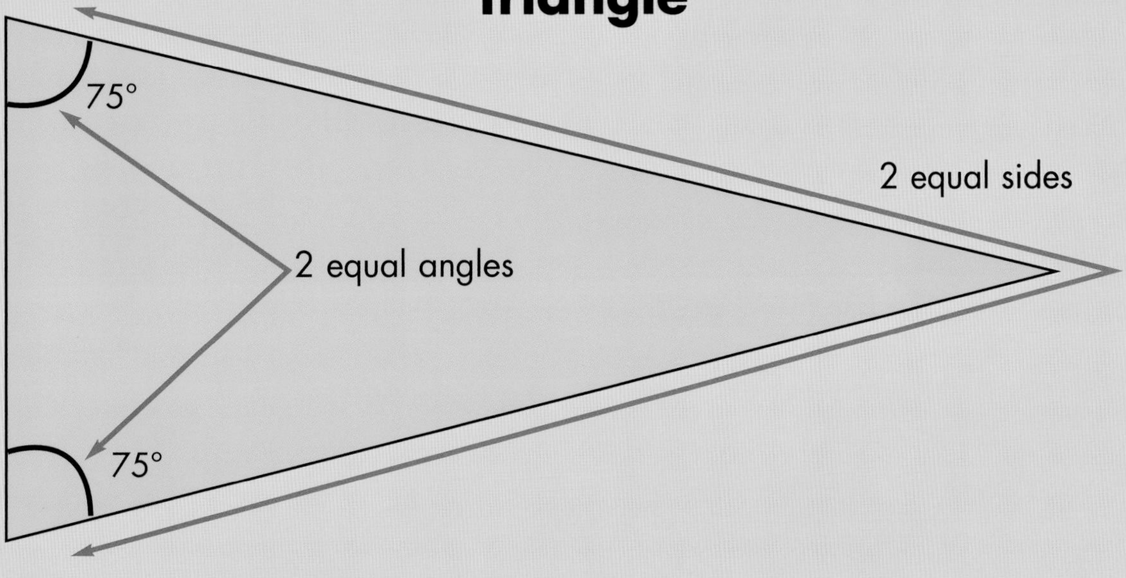

75°

2 equal sides

2 equal angles

75°

Quadrilaterals

Dad explains that **quadrilaterals** all have four sides. They have four vertices. Their sides form four angles. These shapes have all these things in common. Yet, quadrilaterals can look very different. Their sides and angles can be equal or unequal.

Find something that is a quadrilateral. Are any of the sides the same length? Are any of the angles equal?

Activity Box

Which of these shapes are quadrilaterals?

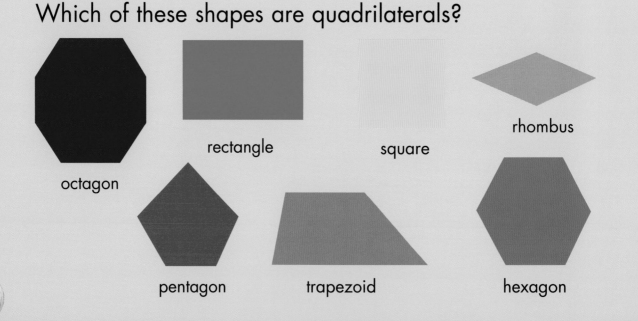

octagon

rectangle

square

rhombus

pentagon

trapezoid

hexagon

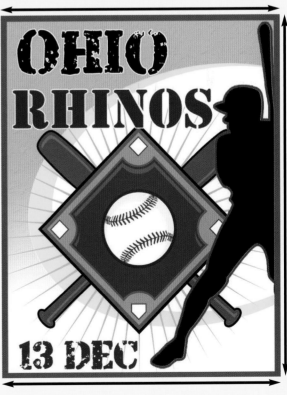

Find the line segments, angles, and quadrilaterals.

Playing Field

Emily points to the shape of the playing field. The bases and home plate are the vertices. There are four of them. The field has four sides. It forms four angles.

She says, "I see a quadrilateral!"

Dad tells her to look closely. The distance from base to base is the same. The sides are the same size. All four angles are equal. They are all right angles. This special shape is also a square.

Activity Box

Get an adult to help you. Spread cream cheese or jam between two pieces of bread. Cut your sandwich into triangles, squares, or other fun polygons!

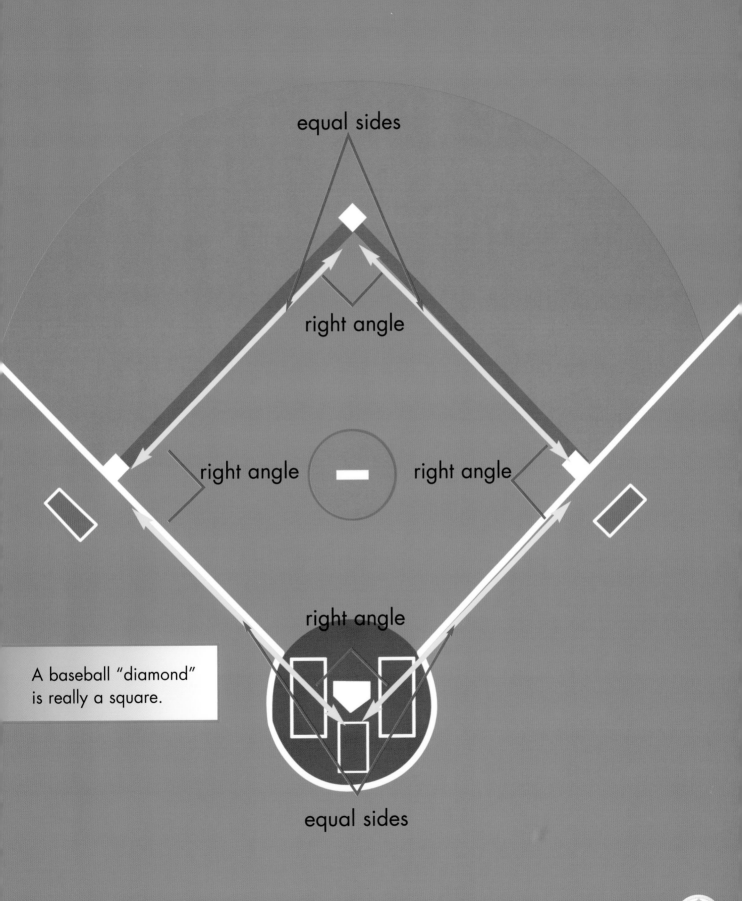

equal sides

right angle

right angle   ━   right angle

right angle

A baseball "diamond"
is really a square.

equal sides

A Base Hit

The batter swings and hits the ball. He runs to first base. Emily can see that first base is a square, too. A square has four equal sides. It has four right angles.

Dad says that a square is a special kind of polygon. It is a **regular polygon**. A regular polygon has sides that are the same length. On a regular polygon, all the angles are equal.

Activity Box

Get some colored construction paper. Cut out several triangles. Cut out several squares. Glue them on another piece of paper to make a polygon picture!

right
angle

side

vertex

square

**equilateral
triangle**

To find a regular
polygon, look for
equal angles and sides.

▲ first base

The Score

Emily looks at the big scoreboard. It is shaped like a **rectangle**. A rectangle is also a polygon. It has four sides and four right angles. It is like a square in those ways. Not all the sides of a rectangle are the same length, however.

A rectangle is an **irregular polygon**. Irregular polygons have sides that are not the same length. Irregular polygons have angles that are not always equal.

Activity Box

Sort the following polygons into two groups. Put regular polygons in one group. Put irregular polygons in the other one.

polygon	irregular polygons	regular polygons

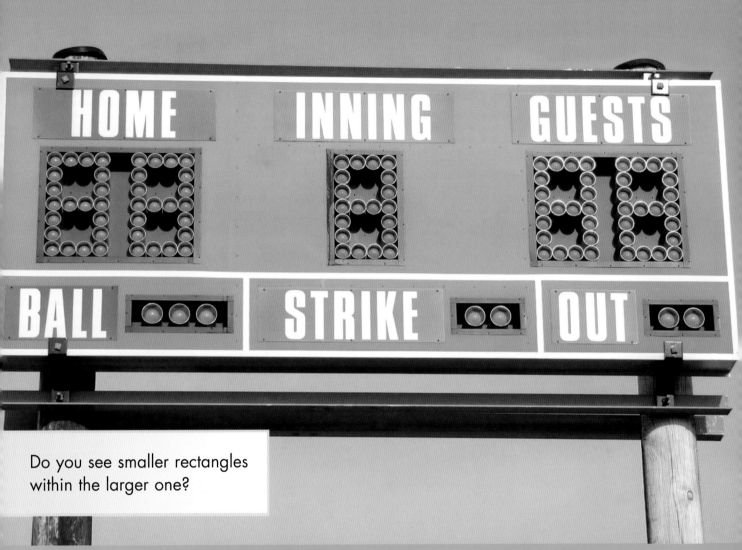

Do you see smaller rectangles within the larger one?

irregular polygons

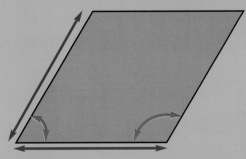

equal sides but
unequal angles

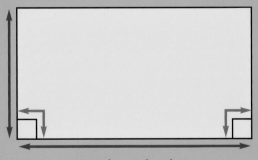

equal angles but
unequal sides

Home Run

The next batter swings. It is a hit! He runs to first base, to second base, and to third base. Then he slides into home plate. It is a home run!

Emily notices that home plate is not shaped like the other bases. It has five sides. It has five vertices. It has five angles. The shape of home plate is called a **pentagon**.

Activity Box

Take a walk around your neighborhood with an adult. Bring a camera or a drawing paper and pencil. Draw or take photos of the polygons you find.

Shapes are everywhere!

▼ home plate

Glossary

acute angles Angles that measure between 0 and 90 degrees

angle A figure formed by two lines that start at a common point

degrees Measures for angles, with 360 degrees around the center of a circle

irregular polygon A polygon whose sides or angles are not equal

length Distance from one point to another, how long something is

line segments Sections of lines which have two endpoints

obtuse angles Angles that measure between 90 and 180 degrees

pentagon Polygon with five sides and five vertices

points Positions in space

polygons Closed shapes made up of at least three straight line segments, in which each line segment connects to just two other line segments

quadrilaterals Polygons that have four sides

rectangle A polygon with four right angles, but four sides that are not equal

regular polygon A polygon with equal angles and equal sides

right angles Angles that measure exactly 90 degrees

sides Lines of a polygon that go from one vertex to another

vertex Point where two line segments meet, sometimes called a corner

vertices More than one vertex

width Distance from one side to another

Index